# PARIS CONFIDENTIAL

## HIDDEN GEMS LOVED BY LOCALS

JONGLEZ PUBLISHING

Travel guides

‘TO BREATHE PARIS
IS TO PRESERVE
ONE’S SOUL’

**VICTOR HUGO**

Paris is my city. I was born here, I grew up here. I often leave, I always come back.

I spend time in its cafés, restaurants, shops, historic places (particularly the secret ones) and even its hotels.

One thing I particularly like about Paris is that you never get bored. It's a perfect city for wandering around at random, with the guarantee that you'll always – and I do mean always – make delightful new discoveries: someone at the neighbouring table in a café I'd like to chat to, a new boutique or bistro, a museum that has redesigned its displays, a new secret spot ...

I've been exploring the streets of my city for over 30 years now. I've written one book about its unusual shops, another about its secret bars and restaurants, and others about its unusual nights and little-known historic places. Only the last of these (*Secret Paris*) is still in print.

As for the rest, it took me a while to decide to distill the essence of my research down to my best finds – the results of a lifetime of wandering. The choices are highly personal, of course. A few secret places slipped in; others are less so. But the common denominator is that I've always come away from them saying to myself, 'Wow, what an exceptional time I've had!' – not just good (otherwise the book would be 1,000 pages long), but truly exceptional. A sort of best of the best of the city. Because Paris abhors mediocrity. Paris deserves the exceptional.

You may not always agree and you may have other suggestions. Don't hesitate to drop me a line. I'll be delighted to continue discovering new places and to add some of them to the next edition.

Enjoy!

Thomas Jonglez
thomasjonglez@editionsjonglez.com

## **WHAT YOU WON'T FIND** IN THIS GUIDE

- A map of the Paris metro
- How to get to Disneyland
- The most boring Michelin-starred restaurants
- The places everyone's talking about on Instagram that will have changed or disappeared six months from now

## **WHAT YOU WILL FIND** IN THIS GUIDE

- How to stargaze at the Sorbonne
- The city's most beautiful libraries
- The loveliest secret spots for kissing in Paris
- The top hôtels de charme where even Parisians sometimes spend the night
- The most romantic walk in Paris
- The most beautiful restaurant in the world?

# THE SYMBOLS OF **PARIS CONFIDENTIAL**

< 20 €

20 to 100 €

> 100 €

Book ahead

Spots for
kissing in Paris

---

Opening times often vary,
so also check the website of the place
you're planning to visit.

01. French chic
02. A magical stroll at the end of the day through the heart of Paris
03. The epitome of Parisian elegance and chic
04. Visiting the city's major museums at night
05. Cruising on the Seine in style
06. Two bistros that haven't changed since the 1950s
07. An evening in Paris's most beautiful theatres
08. The ultimate sound experience
09. Cinema, just like in the good old days
10. In search of Paris' best cocktail bar
11. A hotel with the vibe of a family-run guesthouse from the last cent
12. Stargazing at the Sorbonne
13. The most beautiful libraries in Pari
14. Augustin, culinary artist
15. All the magic of the capital
16. A true cabinet of curiosities
17. A forgotten architectural jewel

18. A few restaurants we really love ...
19. Like the place des Vosges, but without the cars or crowds ...
20. The best baguette in Paris
21. An exceptional pizza
22. One of the capital's greatest architectural surprises
23. The most beautiful restaurant in the world?
24. The coolest thrift store in Paris
25. A cosy bar with British charm
26. Some of the most beautiful lesser-known museums
27. A luxury hotel, like out in the country
28. Experience the sacred soul of Paris
29. Have Montmartre all to yourself
30. The best places for a sweeter side of Paris

PAVILLON DE LA REINE

# #01

# FRENCH **CHIC**

Does the huge number of so-called hôtels de charme in the capital leave your head spinning? Are you looking for a perfectly located (in other words, not near the Champs-Élysées), typically Parisian hotel that epitomises French chic?

Here are four fabulous options.

> **Le Pavillon de la Reine** (Marais, 3rd arrondissement). Its great advantage is that it overlooks the magnificent Place des Vosges. In winter, in the entrance lounges, the fire crackles in the fireplace from breakfast through to dinner, and the space is open to outside guests. In summer, there is a very pleasant terrace in the inner courtyard, as well as a small, charming underground spa with a jacuzzi and hammam.

**LE PAVILLON DE LA REINE**
**28, PLACE DES VOSGES**
**75003 PARIS**

Kiss réservé

| | | |
|---|---|---|
| +33 1 40 29 19 19 | pavillon-de-la-reine.com<br>contact@pdlr.fr | Metro: Chemin Vert |

© DAVID CRIMBERT

© JEROME CALLAND

© DAVID GRIMBERT

PHOTOS © HÔTEL MONTE CRISTO

> **Hôtel Monte Cristo** (Latin Quarter, 5th arrondissement). Very well located at the foot of rue Mouffetard and rue Monge, in a neighbourhood we love, away from the usual tourist crowds. Wonderfully successful colonial-style decor, a swimming pool, a sauna and a warm welcome: Hôtel Monte Cristo has it all, including a bar with around 1,500 different rums.

**HÔTEL MONTE CRISTO**
**20-22, RUE PASCAL**
**75005 PARIS**

+33 1 40 09 09 09

hotelmontecristoparis.com
reservation@hotelmontecristoparis.com
Instagram: @hotelmontecristoparis

Metro:
Censier-Dubenton

> **Hôtel de l'Abbaye** (Saint-Germain-des-Prés, 6th arrondissement), for its timeless classic-chic style, a fireplace where you can sit and enjoy a drink in winter (reserve your spot at the reception), a small garden and the invisible presence of former guests, such as Marcello Mastroianni.

**HÔTEL DE L'ABBAYE**
**10, RUE CASSETTE**
**75006 PARIS**

| | | |
|---|---|---|
| +33 1 45 44 38 11 | hotelabbayeparis.com<br>reception@hotelabbayeparis.com<br>Instagram: @hoteldelabbayeparis | Metro: Saint-Sulpice |

> **Grand Hôtel Cayré** (Saint-Germain-des-Prés, 6th arrondissement). Perfectly located just a few metres from Rue du Bac metro station, a three-minute walk from the Musée d'Orsay and Saint-Germain-des-Prés. Beautiful decor, and a quality restaurant with friendly service that even Parisians come to enjoy. Ask, if possible, for one of the rooms with a small terrace overlooking the Eiffel Tower: quite simply magical when it sparkles at the appointed hour right in front of you.

**LE GRAND HÔTEL CAYRÉ**
**4, BOULEVARD RASPAIL**
**75007 PARIS**

| | | |
|---|---|---|
| +33 1 45 44 38 88 | miirohotels.com/es/legrandhotelcayre<br>reservations@legrandhotelcayre.com<br>Instagram: @legrandhotelcayre | Metro: Saint-Sulpice |

© STUDIO UNFOLDED

© STUDIO UNFOLDED

PHOTOS © JAMES MCDONALD

**LE GRAND HÔTEL CAYRÉ**

#02

# **A MAGICAL STROLL AT THE END OF THE DAY** THROUGH THE HEART OF PARIS

There's no more perfect way to experience the magic of Paris than by going for a relaxing stroll through the centre of the city at the end of the day.

Start in the glorious gardens of the Palais-Royal, surrounded by arcades lined with pretty boutiques – the epitome of Parisian chic.

Grab a free chair and sit by the central fountain or in one of the small, enclosed gardens. Enjoy the moment, watching the comings and goings of Parisians and tourists who are all aware of being in some of the most beautiful surroundings in the world.

Leaving the gardens to the south, you'll find yourself on Place Colette. Turn left to take Passage Richelieu, which runs across the Louvre (make sure to look at the museum's pretty courtyards, visible through a large bay window) and leads to the Pyramid. The outdoor gallery of the beautiful Café Marly under the arcades is the perfect place to enjoy a drink with a view.

Continue left towards the magnificent Cour Carrée (Square Courtyard), which looks spectacular when lit up at night. Sit for a moment on the edge of the central fountain to soak up

the magic of the place before heading out to cross the Pont des Arts pedestrian bridge.

On the other side of the Seine, you have two options: either take Rue Bonaparte to Saint-Germain-des-Prés and the famous Café de Flore or the no less famous Les Deux Magots (which is actually nicer for breakfast before 10am, without the crowds) or continue along the Seine to your left and head towards the tip of the Île de la Cité and the pedestrian quays, where you can sit and dream at the water's edge.

© ABOBE STOCK / VADIM

SAPEURS-POMPIERS
DE PARIS

PHOTOS © STEPHEN KENT JOHNOSON

#03

# THE EPITOME OF **PARISIAN ELEGANCE AND CHIC**

Established in 1996 just around the corner from the Louvre, Astier de Villatte is an exceptional little boutique that many consider the epitome of Parisian elegance and chic.

In a delightful 100% Parisian decor (creaky wooden floors, ancient washbasin in front of an old-fashioned staircase, etc.), you'll find the magnificent handmade ceramics the boutique is known for, as well as perfumes, candles and more.

It's expensive, of course, but sophistication comes at a price ... So why not treat yourself to a plate every now and then, as some people do, to assemble a complete, deliberately mismatched set over time?

**ASTIER DE VILLATTE**
**173, RUE SAINT-HONORÉ**
**75001 PARIS**

Mon-Sat: 11am / 7pm | astierdevillatte.com | Metro: Pyramides, Tuileries ou Palais-Royal - Musée du Louvre

COU URS VERNIS BROSSERIE

RUE SAINT-HONORÉ
A. V.
PARIS

Paris
A dozen roses

# #04

# VISITING THE CITY'S MAJOR MUSEUMS AT NIGHT

Paris, like many other cities in the world, suffers from over-tourism. The sometimes disrespectful crowds that descend on museums like the Louvre and the Musée d'Orsay inevitably ruin the experience a little.

The best way to see the world's most beautiful museums and some of the city's other gems is to visit them at night.

The Louvre on Fridays, the Musée d'Orsay on Thursdays: you'll find all the magic of their collections – and the night adds an extra layer of mystery, perfect for a solitary visit or for luring in a passing tourist. Not to mention that once the sun goes down, strange things sometimes happen in museums, like the man we saw stepping over the security cordons and surreptitiously throwing himself on a Babylonian tombstone to absorb its energy – an instant stolen from eternity.

**MUSÉE D'ORSAY** – Thursday until 9:45pm
**MUSÉE DU LOUVRE** – Friday until 9pm
**MUSÉE DES ARTS ET MÉTIERS** – Friday until 9pm
**MUSÉE D'ART MODERNE DE PARIS** – Thursday until 9:30pm for temporary exhibitions
**BOURSE DU COMMERCE** – Friday until 9pm
**MUSÉE DES ARTS DÉCORATIFS** – Thursday until 9pm

© AAROM ORE - UNSPLASH

#05

# CRUISING ON THE SEINE IN STYLE

Have you always thought that cruising on the Seine could be great, but that the Bateaux Mouches, with their hordes of tourists and pre-recorded announcements blaring over loudspeakers, just weren't for you?

We get it.

Since 2021, Le Bateau Français has had the good idea of offering a 90-minute 'chic' cruise with champagne and everything you need for a festive or romantic experience – your choice. All on a magnificent, luxurious retro 30s-style boat, made in France in La Rochelle.

**LE BATEAU FRANÇAIS**

| | | |
|---|---|---|
| Closed from mid-January to mid-March. From 1 to 8 passengers | lebateaufrancais.com<br>contact@lebateaufrancais.com | Boarding at: Louvre, Musée d'Orsay, Port des Champs-Élysées or Saint-Germain-des-Prés |

© WEBSTYLESTORY

PELFORTH

# #06

# TWO BISTROS THAT HAVEN'T CHANGED **SINCE THE 1950S**

> **Au Petit Bar** (1st arrondissement): Tucked away just 100 metres from Rue Saint-Honoré and its luxury shops, Au Petit Bar is such an unusual place in Paris that many of the locals don't even know about it.

No Wi-Fi, no credit cards, a decor that's remained unchanged for decades, a warm welcome, quality home-cooked food at very reasonable prices – and even a phone from the 1980s on the counter that actually works ...

The menu includes a few classic starters and a single dish of the day, which changes daily: salt pork with lentils, roast beef with homemade fries, and so on. Round off your meal with a dessert and voilà – you'll have a great time in a friendly atmosphere where everyone talks to everyone else.

**AU PETIT BAR**
**7, RUE DU MONT THABOR**
**75001 PARIS**

+33 1 42 60 62 09

Metro: Tuileries

© GAELLEFUZET

> **Le Vaudésir** (14th arrondissement)**:** Located far away from the touristy areas, Le Vaudésir is a genuinely old-fashioned bistro: period decor (early 20th century), daily specials for €8.90, home-cooked food and a no-frills atmosphere with everyone talking to each other, encouraged by the welcoming owner ... Truly our kind of place.

If the Paris of yesteryear is what you're looking for, you'll find it here, just a stone's throw from the Hôpital Sainte-Anne.

**LE VAUDÉSIR**
**41, RUE DAREAU**
**75014 PARIS**

+33 1 43 22 03 93

Metro: Saint-Jacques or Mouton-Duvernet

© PIERRICK BOURGAULT

ENTREES

> **Le Bar Fleuri** (19th arrondissement)**:** Just a stone's throw from Parc des Buttes-Chaumont, perfect for a walk to digest lunch, Le Bar Fleuri is something of an endangered species: a warm, popular, old-school neighbourhood restaurant with unbeatable value for money. The standout is the free-range chicken with fries for €6.86, which is a better choice than some of the other dishes on the menu, which are considerably more expensive. Better, more pleasant and cheaper than the ultra-touristy bouillons in other parts of Paris.

That said, avoid Saturday lunch: the queue can feel a little too long...

**LE BAR FLEURI**
**1, RUE DU PLATEAU**
**75019 PARIS**

| | | |
|---|---|---|
| +33 1 42 08 13 38 | Instagram: @fleuribar | Metro: Buttes Chaumont |

# #07

# AN EVENING IN PARIS'S **MOST BEAUTIFUL THEATRES**

Whilst everyone knows the magnificent Opéra Garnier, where spending an evening is always magical, the general public is less aware of the impressive number of Parisian theatres worth visiting for their spectacular architecture alone.

Among these, we strongly recommend booking an evening at the Théâtre du Palais-Royal (opened in 1783), the Théâtre des Champs-Élysées (1913) or the Opéra-Comique (1714), as well as two lesser-known venues: the Théâtre de la Renaissance (1873) and the Théâtre Louis Jouvet (1894).

For readers who don't speak French, the Opéra Garnier, Opéra-Comique and Théâtre Louis Jouvet stage operas, concerts and ballets that can be fully enjoyed even without understanding the language.

**THÉÂTRE DU PALAIS-ROYAL**
**38, RUE DE MONTPENSIER**
**75001 PARIS**

réservé

| | | |
|---|---|---|
| +33 1 42 97 40 00 | theatrepalaisroyal.com | Metro: Pyramides |

THÉÂTRE DES CHAMPS-ÉLYSÉES

OPÉRA-COMIQUE

IRON CURTAIN. ORDERED FROM ALWYNE DE DARDEL

**OPÉRA-COMIQUE**
**1, PLACE BOIELDIEU**
**75002 PARIS**

*réservé*

+33 1 70 23 01 31
opera-comique.com
Metro: Opéra

**THÉÂTRE**
**DES CHAMPS-ÉLYSÉES**
**15, AVENUE MONTAIGNE**
**75008 PARIS**

*réservé*

+33 1 49 52 50 50
theatrechampselysees.fr
Metro: Alma-Marceau

THÉÂTRE DE LA RENAISSANCE

THÉÂTRE LOUIS JOUVET

**THÉÂTRE LOUIS JOUVET**
**2-4, SQUARE**
**DE L'OPÉRA-LOUIS JOUVET**
**75009 PARIS**

*réservé*

+33 1 53 05 19 19
athenee-theatre.com
Metro: Opéra

**THÉÂTRE**
**DE LA RENAISSANCE**
**20, BOULEVARD SAINT-MARTIN**
**75010 PARIS**

*réservé*

+33 1 42 08 18 50
theatredelarenaissance.com
Metro: Strasbourg-Saint-Denis

THÉÂTRE LOUIS JOUVET

OPÉRA-COMIQUE

# #08

# **THE ULTIMATE SOUND** EXPERIENCE

Far from trendy music bars, Listener is a rare place where music truly sits at the heart of everything.

On the ground floor, the bar space hosts DJ sets on Saturday evenings and Sunday afternoons at 4pm. Behind the bar, you'll find several booths for 'musical naps'. Settle into a plush armchair with high-fidelity headphones and listen to your own favourites or discover the owners' recommendations.

But the real magic happens downstairs. Here, you can book a proper listening room with exceptional professional-grade equipment in extraordinary conditions, including two giant speakers imported from Greece, a 120-kilo valve amplifier straight from Cyprus, and a turntable with twin tonearms.

**LISTENER**
**10, RUE VIVIENNE**
**75002 PARIS**

| | | |
|---|---|---|
| Musical nap: €15 for 30 minutes<br>Listening room: €50 to €100 per hour<br>DJ sets Saturday evenings and Sundays at 4pm | +33 9 78 81 17 21<br>listener.fr<br>Events announced on Instagram: @listener_paris | Metro: Bourse |

# #09

# CINEMA, **JUST LIKE IN THE GOOD OLD DAYS**

Tired of microscopic cinemas? Feeling nostalgic for the era of the silver screen when cinemas had a capacity of 2,000 to 3,000 seats – or more – and a trip to the cinema still meant going to a show?

Then head over to the Grand Rex, one of the few cinemas in the world that survive from this golden age. Since Paris is lucky enough to be home to it, you should definitely not miss out!

Opened in 1931 and listed in 1981, the large Screen 1 (avoid the other screens, obviously) has a capacity of 2,700. In 1960, it had more visitors than the Louvre.

In addition to the main screen and its 'Mediterranean/antique' city decor, with coloured walls that echo the Art Deco ambience of villas on the Côte d'Azur, make sure to check out the magnificent frescoes on the walls of the staircases and along the corridors leading to the main screen, which most cinema-goers overlook.

**LE GRAND REX**
**1, BOULEVARD POISSONNIÈRE**
**75002 PARIS**

legrandrex.com

Metro: Bonne-Nouvelle

REX
AVATAR
REX
BAR
LE GRAND REX
AVATAR
LE 14 DÉCEMBRE AU CINÉMA

© DIMITRI BOURRIAU

#10

# IN SEARCH OF PARIS' **BEST COCKTAIL BARS**

Cocktail bars are now plentiful in Paris, but which ones are genuinely good addresses where the bartenders truly know their craft and pursue it with passion? Some, sadly, seem more interested in their Instagram follower count...

In the heart of the city, you can't overlook **Harry's Bar**, a Parisian institution. This legendary spot has serious history: it's where the Bloody Mary was invented. The moment you step through the door, dark wood panelling and leather banquettes welcome you into a hushed atmosphere where time seems to stand still.

**HARRY'S BAR**
**5, RUE DAUNOU**
**75002 PARIS**

harrysbar.com
Instagram: @harrysbar_theoriginal

Metro: Opéra

Harry's New York Bar
Harry's BAR
VIET
THAÏ

B.O.B

© I. MATHIE

Want something a bit edgier? Near Strasbourg-Saint-Denis, **Copper Bay** offers a relaxed vibe, as does **Classique**, hidden behind the discreet door of a former pharmacy. By day, it's a café like any other, but when night falls, a subtle magic takes hold. The atmosphere shifts, and the neighbourhood bistro transforms into a cocktail bar where experimentation and happy-hour oysters reign supreme. Perfect with friends or a loved one at any time of day.

**COPPERBAY**
**5, RUE BOUCHARDON**
**75010 PARIS**

copperbay.fr
Instagram: @copperbay_paris
Metro: Strasbourg-Saint-Denis

**CLASSIQUE**
**1 BIS, RUE LALLIER**
**75009 PARIS**

Instagram: @classique.cafe
Metro: Pigalle

Finally, steps from the Palais-Royal, **Danico** hides behind the doors of trattoria Daroco. Each season, the top-notch cocktail menu changes and whisks you off to a new destination.

**DANICO**
**6, RUE VIVIENNE**
**75002 PARIS**

daroco.com/danico
Instagram: @danicoparis

Metro: Bourse

#11

# A HOTEL WITH THE VIBE OF A FAMILY-RUN **GUESTHOUSE FROM THE LAST CENTURY**

Located in the heart of the Latin Quarter, the Hôtel des Grandes Écoles is a little gem that looks a lot like a family-run guesthouse from the last century.

Standing outside the high doors facing the street, you'd never guess what's hidden behind them: a cobbled alleyway lined with charming one-storey houses, all in a lush green setting that's rare in Paris. Having breakfast on the terrace under the trees in fine weather is a pure delight.

There's only one slight drawback: some of the beautiful rooms, with their old-fashioned decor, are quite small. But you can hardly expect a three-star hotel to be a palace ...

**HÔTEL DES GRANDES ÉCOLES**
**75, RUE DU CARDINAL LEMOINE**
**75005 PARIS**

Kiss réservé

+33 1 43 26 79 23 | hoteldesgrandesecoles.com | Metro: Cardinal Lemoine

# #12

# **STARGAZING** AT THE SORBONNE

It's one of central Paris's best-kept secrets. Twice a week, on Monday and Friday after sunset, five lucky individuals are granted access to the Sorbonne Observatory for an extraordinary evening: observing the moon and the heavens from the heart of Paris, with a guide from the Société Astronomique de France (French Astronomical Society).

Spend an unforgettable evening gazing up at the stars in a timeless atmosphere that could be straight out of *Tintin and the Shooting Star*.

Tickets to this magical experience are hard to come by, so don't miss your chance to book a spot: at the end of each month, you can make reservations for the following month.

**OBSERVATOIRE DE LA SORBONNE**
**17, RUE DE LA SORBONNE**
**75005 PARIS**

Mon & Fri: depending on when the sun sets

boutique.saf-astronomie.fr/produit/visite-de-lobservatoire-de-la-sorbonne

Metro: Cluny-La Sorbonne

MACHIAVEL
1469-1527

# #13

# THE MOST BEAUTIFUL LIBRARIES
## IN PARIS

If you've never been a student at a Parisian university, you've probably never seen inside any of the city's libraries. Which is a shame because they're among the most beautiful in the world, with architecture to rival that of any museum and the advantage that (in most cases) you can enter free of charge just by presenting your ID. So there's really nothing to stop you from sitting there for a while, just soaking up the atmosphere.

The only exception is the sublime Salle Labrouste at the Bibliothèque Nationale's Richelieu site (2nd arrondissement), which has recently been renovated and is reserved for researchers. That said, you can take a peek inside from the entrance (except on Sundays).

**BIBLIOTHÈQUE NATIONALE DE FRANCE (RICHELIEU SITE)**
**5, RUE VIVIENNE**
**75002 PARIS**

**Salle Labrouste**
**(1861-1868)**
Opening days and times: bnf.fr

**Salle Ovale**
**(1897-1932)**
Opening days and times: bnf.fr

+33 1 53 79 59 59
Metro: Bourse

© PECCADILLE

© JOËL GALERAN

**BIBLIOTHÈQUE DE L'HÔTEL DE VILLE (1890)**
**5, RUE LOBAU**
**75004 PARIS**

Sat & Sun: closed

Metro: Hôtel de Ville

**BIBLIOTHÈQUE SAINTE GENEVIÈVE (1851)**
**10, PLACE DU PANTHÉON**
**75005 PARIS**

| | | |
|---|---|---|
| Sun: closed | +33 1 44 41 97 97<br>bsg.univ-paris3.fr | Metro: Cluny-La Sorbonne |

**BIBLIOTHÈQUE INTERUNIVERSITAIRE DE LA SORBONNE (1770) ▲**
**17, RUE DE LA SORBONNE**
**75005 PARIS**

| | | |
|---|---|---|
| Sun: closed | +33 1 40 46 30 97<br>Access restricted to students, teachers, researchers and publishers | Metro: Maubert-Mutualité |

**BIBLIOTHÈQUE MAZARINE (1643)**
**23, QUAI DE CONTI**
**75006 PARIS**

| | | |
|---|---|---|
| Sun: closed | +33 1 44 41 44 06<br>bibliotheque-mazarine.fr | Metro: Pont Neuf |

**BIBLIOTHÈQUE DU SÉNAT (1841)**
**15, RUE VAUGIRARD**
**75006 PARIS**

| | | |
|---|---|---|
| Open on European Heritage Days | With a 52-metre gallery and ceiling paintings by Delacroix | Metro: Odéon |

**ANNEXE DE LA BIBLIOTHÈQUE DU SÉNAT (1642)**
**15, RUE VAUGIRARD**
**75006 PARIS**

| | | |
|---|---|---|
| Open on European Heritage Days | The building housed Europe's first museum in the mid-18th century | Metro: Odéon |

**BIBLIOTHÈQUE HISTORIQUE DE L'ÉCOLE DE MÉDECINE (1891)** ▼
**12, RUE DE L'ÉCOLE DE MÉDECINE**
**75006 PARIS**

| | |
|---|---|
| Sun: closed | Metro: Odéon |

© MARIE-LAN NGUYEN

©ADOBE STOCK / DBRNJHRJ

MAZARINAEA

AUGUSTIN
MARCHAND D'VINS

NUL
n'est
censé
ignorer
la loire

AUGUSTIN
MARCHAND D'VINS

# #14

## **AUGUSTIN,**
## CULINARY ARTIST

You can count Parisian restaurants like this on the fingers of one hand: more than simply lunch or dinner, Augustin Marchand d'Vins offers a true experience in every sense of the word.

A former resident of the Villa Medici, where he was employed as a culinary artist, Augustin has retained his appreciation of quality and good presentation from his time in Rome. On four evenings a week (Thursday to Sunday), guests are served one dish, and one dish only, which is a genuine artistic creation. Beware: there won't be enough for everyone!

In this intimate setting, the high-quality cuisine enhanced by a fanciful je ne sais quoi just adds to the delight.

Not to be missed!

**AUGUSTIN MARCHAND D'VINS**
**26, RUE DES GRANDS AUGUSTINS**
**75006 PARIS**

réservé

| | | |
|---|---|---|
| +33 9 81 21 76 21 | augustinmarchand.com<br>Instagram: @augustin75006 | Metro: Odéon |

# #15

# ALL THE MAGIC
OF THE CAPITAL

Most Parisians – let alone tourists – don't often think of going into the École des beaux-arts. Which is a shame because, thanks to the frequent exhibitions held there, it's often possible to get in and linger for a while in the school's uniquely romantic atmosphere.

Between the many copies of famous artworks to be seen here and there, work by students from all eras (recent and not so recent), the eclectic architecture of the various buildings, the magnificent Palais des Études and the remarkable Florentine-style cloister in the Cour des Mûriers (Mulberry Courtyard), you'll feel you can almost touch the magic of the capital.

Don't miss the chapel of the former monastery of the Petits Augustins friars when it's open.

**ÉCOLE DES BEAUX-ARTS DE PARIS**
**14, RUE BONAPARTE**
**75006 PARIS**

| | | |
|---|---|---|
| Open for exhibitions and organised events, such as European Heritage Days (September), information days (early February) and open studios days (last weekend in June) | +33 1 47 03 50 74<br>beauxartsparis.fr | Metro:<br>Saint-Germain-des-Prés |

© HERMANN WENDLER

© SELBYMAY

#16

# A TRUE **CABINET OF CURIOSITIES**

Some people come here as if they were visiting a natural history museum or a cabinet of curiosities, and that's fine.

Others come to treat themselves: a stuffed lion or zebra for the hallway, a meteorite or a chunk of Mars for the coffee table or, for those with more limited budgets, a magnificent butterfly with azure wings ...

Unless of course you opt for a polar bear, a crocodile, an iridescent beetle, a spider or (more wisely) a herbarium press or one of the famous educational posters that made the company such a success in the late 19th century.

Founded in 1831 in a magnificent town house built between 1697 and 1699, the venerable Deyrolle is still the go-to place in France for taxidermy and entomology.

**DEYROLLE**
**46, RUE DU BAC**
**75007 PARIS**

+33 1 42 22 30 07

deyrolle.com
Instagram: @deyrolle.officiel

Metro: Rue du Bac

© MARC DANTAN

# #17

# A FORGOTTEN **ARCHITECTURAL JEWEL**

Are you desperate for some peace and quiet after being jostled by the tourist hordes in the grands magasins? Or do you simply happen to be in the Opéra district, completely unaware that there's an architectural jewel hidden just around the corner? Located a short walk away, on Boulevard Haussmann, it's one of Paris's biggest secrets: the historic headquarters of Société Générale, founded in 1912.

When the bank is open (because, yes, the main office is still in operation and continues to serve customers), saunter in and admire the spectacular circular counter (known as *le fromage*, 'the cheese') under an enormous glass dome with a steel frame (24 metres in diameter) designed by Jacques Galland.

The magnificent mosaic floors were created by Alphonse Gentil and François-Eugène Bourdet. In the basement, take a peek at the main armoured door to the vault, which is 40 cm thick and weighs 18 tonnes.

But remember to be discreet – this is, after all, first and foremost a place of work.

**HISTORICAL HEADQUARTERS OF SOCIÉTÉ GÉNÉRALE**
**29, BOULEVARD HAUSSMANN**
**75009 PARIS**

| Sun: closed | Also open on heritage days | Metro: Chaussée d'Antin - La Fayette |
|---|---|---|

# #18

# A FEW RESTAURANTS **WE REALLY LOVE...**

Even in Paris, there are surprisingly few restaurants where you can enjoy a truly exceptional meal. Too expensive, dull, like so many gastronomic restaurants, with bland decor, questionable service and reservations that are almost impossible to secure...

Here is our small, admittedly subjective selection.

> **Chez Georges** (2nd arrondissement)

Far from passing trends, Chez Georges occasionally attracts a few celebrities, drawn among other things by its delicious pavé du mail, a beef fillet with mustard, butter, cream and cognac sauce, as well as by its historic decor, handwritten menu and the large painting at the entrance, signed by J.C. Mathon in 1961.

At times, you may find yourself sitting a little too close to the neighbouring tables, but that can also lead to a few words being exchanged with their occupants. In summer, the terrace spreads greedily across Place des Petits-Pères.

**CHEZ GEORGES**
**1, RUE DU MAIL**
**75002 PARIS**

+33 1 42 60 07 11 | Metro: Bourse

© DAN ASSAYAG

> **Billili** (10th arrondissement)

We love everything about Billili: the decor (simple and tasteful), the food (excellent; one or two real dishes but mainly tapas), the atmosphere (lively and cheerful), the service (friendly), the prices (very reasonable) and also the fact that they don't take reservations. Apart from the obvious drawback of not being able to guarantee you'll get a table there in the evening (it's easier at lunchtime), this means that you can stop by for lunch or dinner on a whim, unlike at most other (good) restaurants in the capital. Long live spontaneity! Of course, to get seated for dinner without having to wait until 10pm, you'll have to arrive on the early side (around 7:30pm) ...

**RESTAURANT BILLILI**
**136, RUE DU FAUBOURG POISSONNIÈRE**
**75010 PARIS**

No reservations

Metro: Poissonnière, Gare-du-Nord or Barbès-Rochechouart

> **Erso** (11th arrondissement)

Its lovely décor, inventive, high-quality cooking, extremely reasonable prices and friendly welcome make this restaurant an exceptional address and a real favourite of ours.

**ERSO**
**18, RUE SAINT-AMBROISE**
**75011 PARIS**

réservé

| | | |
|---|---|---|
| +33 1 81 69 96 55 | erso-restaurant.fr<br>Instagram: @erso.restaurant | Metro: Saint-Ambroise or Rue Saint-Maur |

PHOTOS © OLIVIER-PLACET.COM

© _PEPA

> **Godaille** (12th arrondissement)

Overlooking the charming Square Trousseau, Godaille is the kind of place that gets everything right. The welcome is warm, the décor inviting, the atmosphere convivial, and above all, the food is excellent. It offers a short menu, but every dish here counts. The bread is delicious too! Ideal for soaking up every last bit of sauce.

**GODAILLE**
**9, RUE ANTOINE VOLLON**
**75012 PARIS**

réservé

restaurantgodaille.fr
Instagram: @godaille_paris12

Metro: Ledru-Rollin

© _PEPA

© SOCES

> **Soces** (19th arrondissement)

Way up in the northeast of Paris, Soces is genuinely worth the journey, even if you're based on the other side of the city. The setting is friendly, the welcome warm, the cooking truly delicious and inventive, and prices remain reasonable. The fish- and seafood-focused menu changes regularly, but the team always keeps one brilliant starter on offer: an oyster paired with a shot of margarita. The perfect way to start the evening.

**SOCES**
**32, RUE DE LA VILETTE**
**75019 PARIS**

réservé

+33 1 40 34 14 30

soces.fr
Instagram: @soces_paris

Metro: Jourdain

> **Dandelion** (20th arrondissement)

In the east of Paris, on the corner of a quiet square that feels more like a village than the capital (we're rather fond of this part of the 20th arrondissement), Dandelion is the kind of place you'd love to have at the end of your street. The décor is smart and modern, the welcome genuinely warm, and the food consistently good. What more could you want?

**DANDELION**
**6, RUE DES VIGNOLES**
**75020 PARIS**

réservé

| | | |
|---|---|---|
| +33 1 42 50 01 55 | restaurantdandelion.com<br>Instagram: @restaurant.dandelion | Metro: Buzenval |

© HENRY SALOMÉ

# #19

## **LIKE THE PLACE DES VOSGES,** BUT WITHOUT THE CARS OR CROWDS ...

When you need to escape the noise and bustle of the capital, there's a gorgeous and unexpected spot in the 10th arrondissement that's perfect for a quiet break.

Some people describe the magnificent inner courtyard of the old Hôpital Saint-Louis as a Place des Vosges ... without the cars or the crowds. Which gives you a pretty good idea of just how charming and beautiful it is.

Now a listed historic monument, the old hospital was built in response to the great plague epidemic of 1562, which killed more than 68,000 people in Paris.

The flowerbeds in the centre of the lawn were designed to evoke a Maltese cross. Today, one of the hospital's pavilions is home to the Order of Malta, an ancient hospitaller order.

**COURTYARD OF THE OLD HÔPITAL SAINT-LOUIS**
**40, RUE BICHAT ET 1, AVENUE CLAUDE VELLEFAUX**
**75010 PARIS**

Kiss

| | | |
|---|---|---|
| Open every day | +33 1 42 49 49 49 | Metro: Goncourt or Jacques Bonsergent |

SITHAMPARAPPILLAI JEGATHEEPAN, ARTISAN BAKER AT FOURNIL DIDOT

# #20

# THE BEST BAGUETTE IN PARIS

If you aren't lucky enough to live near a top bakery or, worse still, if you don't live in Paris, you're missing out on one of life's greatest pleasures: enjoying a baguette that's so good you can eat it like cake, without butter or jam.

To experience this, we recommend choosing one of the bakeries that feature in the annual competition for the best baguette in Paris. You can't go wrong.

Listed by UNESCO as part of the Intangible Cultural Heritage of Humanity, the baguette is the French symbol par excellence. Up to six billion are produced annually in France. Every year, between 150 and 200 Parisian bakeries participate in a competition to determine the city's ten best baguettes.

Beyond the glory of carrying the day, the winner is given the great honour of becoming official supplier to the President of the Republic and the Élysée Palace for a year.

In other words, if you stop by the winning bakery, you can enjoy the same baguette as the president and his usual distinguished coterie of guests.

Participating bakers must adhere to the following requirements: they must produce 40 baguettes for the competition, each between 50 and 55 cm long, weighing between 250 and 270 grams and containing no more than 18 grams of salt per kilo of flour.

## IN 2026, THE TOP TEN WINNERS WERE:

1. **LE FOURNIL DIDOT** - 103, rue Didot (14th arr.)
2. **BOULANGERIE B&S NATION** - 24, place de la Nation (12th arr.)
3. **L'ÉCRIN GOURMAND** - 15, avenue du Dr Arnold Netter (12th arr.)
4. **MAISON DAGUET** - 175, rue de la Convention (15th arr.)
5. **BOULANGERIE LAURENT B.** - 112, rue Saint-Dominique (7th arr.)
6. **BOULANGERIE GUYOT FERREIRA** - 28, rue Monge (5th arr.)
7. **MAISON LEPARQ** - 6, rue de Lourmel (15th arr.)
8. **BOULANGERIE MODERNE RABINEAU** - 16, rue des Fossés Saint-Jacques (5th arr.)
9. **AUX DÉLICES DE GLACIÈRE** - 90, boulevard Auguste Blanqui (13th arr.)
10. **AU PARADIS DU GOURMAND** - 156, rue Raymond Losserand (14th arr.)

© GUILLAUME BONTEMPS/VILLE DE PARIS

© SHUTTERSTOCK

# #21

# AN EXCEPTIONAL **PIZZA**

The last time we were truly blown away by pizza was in Rome, at Seu Pizza Illuminati, ranked in the top 10 pizzerias worldwide (and featured in our Rome guide from the same collection).

At Oobatz, the pizza selection is small and prices are high, but the dough is exceptional—perfectly crisp—and the toppings are original and beautifully thought through. This is a world away from the common four-cheese or ham-and-cheese pizza.

We have particularly fond memories of a pizza topped with wafer-thin potato slices and preserved lemon, though sadly it's not always on the menu.

Don't miss it!

**OOBATZ**
**4 BIS, AVENUE JEAN AICARD**
**75011 PARIS**

oobatz.fr
Instagram: @o.o.b.a.t.z

Metro: Rue Saint-Maur or Ménilmontant

© OOBATZ

# 22

# ONE OF THE CAPITAL'S **GREATEST ARCHITECTURAL SURPRISES**

Located off the beaten tourist track, the Palais de la Porte-Dorée is nonetheless one of Paris's greatest architectural surprises.

In addition to the enormous bas-relief that adorns the facade, don't miss the central hall (known as the Forum), with its exceptional frescoes painted by Pierre-Henri Ducos de La Haille on the theme of the French colonies. The juxtaposition of these frescoes and the equally magnificent mosaic floor makes for a truly spectacular ensemble.

**PALAIS DE LA PORTE-DORÉE**
**293, AVENUE DAUMESNIL**
**75012 PARIS**

| | | |
|---|---|---|
| Mon: closed | +33 1 53 59 58 60<br>Visit of the central hall and glimpse of the two oval salons: free | Metro: Porte Dorée |

Built by French architect Albert Laprade for the Paris Colonial Exposition of 1931, the Palais de la Porte-Dorée also boasts two beautiful Art Deco oval salons on either side of the entrance hall. They once served as the offices of the colonial administrator, Hubert Lyautey.

# #23

# **THE MOST BEAUTIFUL RESTAURANT** IN THE WORLD?

Built for the 1900 Paris Exposition, Le Train Bleu is arguably the most beautiful restaurant in Paris, if not the world.

Decorated with paintings showing the various destinations of the trains departing from the Gare de Lyon, it is housed within the station itself, on the first floor in front of the main platforms.

Oddly enough, many Parisians – never mind tourists – don't know about it. And yet it exerts such fascination that some regulars even make the round-trip journey by train from Dijon or Lyon in a single day just to go there for lunch ...

The classic French cuisine is decent, though priced too high for the quality on offer, but that's not why you come ...

Bask in the atmosphere and admire the decor and you'll have an excellent time, making it well worth arriving early if you have an afternoon or evening train to catch.

**LE TRAIN BLEU**
**1ST FLOOR, GARE DE LYON**
**PLACE LOUIS ARMAND, HALL 1**
**75012 PARIS**

réservé

| | | |
|---|---|---|
| +33 1 43 43 09 06<br>le-train-bleu.com | Reservations are essential | Metro and RER: Gare de Lyon |

© ADOBE STOCK / KOVALENKOVPETR

TRAIN
BLEU

PENITENCIER DES SALES VOLEURS

Les sales
voleurs

#
24

# THE COOLEST THRIFT STORE IN PARIS

Pénitencier des Sales Voleurs (Dirty Thieves' Penitentiary): the storefront sets the tone ...

Whether in the 20th, 15th or 5th arrondissement, Les Sales Voleurs are thrift stores with a pretty crazy decor (prison, bank or cave, depending on the location) where you can find clothes at prices that change every day.

The entire stock is replaced on Fridays and Sundays, so those are the days when the prices are highest – but also when you get the most choice.

For some really great bargains, go on a Thursday, when everything is just €0.95.

| | | |
|---|---|---|
| **FRIPERIES LES SALES VOLEURS 285, RUE DE VAUGIRARD 75015 PARIS** | **42, RUE MONGE 75005 PARIS** | **31, RUE D'AVRON 75020 PARIS** |
| Instagram: @les.sales.voleurs<br>Metro: Vaugirard | Metro: Cardinal Lemoine | Metro: Buzenval |

#25

# A COSY BAR
## WITH BRITISH CHARM

The library-bar in the magnificent Hôtel Saint-James is a charming and elegant little gem that even many Parisians haven't been to, thinking that it's a private club. Yet the bar is open to the public in the evenings from 7pm.

Wooden floors, antique carpets, comfortable leather and velvet armchairs, a coffered ceiling, bookcases with a spiral staircase on one side and large windows overlooking the garden on the other – the decor of this bar, with its typically British, hushed ambience, verges on perfection.

The intimate atmosphere is perfect for a romantic rendezvous. And if everything goes according to plan, you can always book a room in the hotel to finish off the evening ...

It's also the ideal place to sit and read quietly. In summer, you can enjoy a drink in the charming garden, accompanied by a short à la carte menu.

**LIBRARY-BAR OF THE HÔTEL SAINT-JAMES**
**5, PLACE DU CHANCELIER ADENAUER**
**75116 PARIS**

Kiss réservé

Daily: 8:30am / midnight for hotel members and guests
Daily: 7pm / midnight for the general public

+33 1 44 05 81 81
contact@saint-james-paris.com
Instagram: @saintjamesparis

Metro: Porte Dauphine

© CELINE YLMZ – UNSPLASH

# #26

# SOME OF THE MOST BEAUTIFUL **LESSER-KNOWN MUSEUMS**

Paris may have some of the finest museums in the world, but it's best to avoid the Louvre and the Musée d'Orsay during the day, when they're overrun with tourists. If you don't want to wait until nighttime (see page 84), one option is to visit the city's smaller museums that don't attract the crowds. Some are absolutely magnificent and guarantee an authentic, off-the-beaten-track experience.

Our favourites: the Musée Gustave Moreau (9th arrondissement) for its atmosphere and wonderful staircase; the Musée Nissim de Camondo (8th arrondissement) for the beauty of the town house, its 19th-century collections and its historic kitchens; the Musée Bourdelle (15th arrondissement) for the artist's magnificent studio and the sculptures scattered around the garden; and the Musée Jean-Jacques Henner (17th arrondissement).

At the Musée Nissim de Camondo, take advantage of the restaurant located in a beautiful inner courtyard next to the museum.

**MUSÉE GUSTAVE MOREAU**
**14, RUE CATHERINE DE LA ROCHEFOUCAULD**
**75009 PARIS**

| | | |
|---|---|---|
| Tue: closed | +33 1 83 62 78 72<br>musee-moreau.fr<br>Instagram: @museegustavemoreau | Metro:<br>Trinité - d'Estienne d'Orves |

**MUSÉE NISSIM DE CAMONDO**
**63, RUE DE MONCEAU**
**75008 PARIS**

| | | |
|---|---|---|
| Work in progress, reopening in 2030 | +33 1 53 89 06 50<br>madparis.fr/Musee-Nissim-de-Camondo-125 | Metro: Villiers |

© HARTL-MEYER

© HARTL-MEYER

**MUSÉE NATIONAL JEAN-JACQUES HENNER**
**43, AVENUE DE VILLIERS**
**75017 PARIS**

| | | |
|---|---|---|
| Tue: closed | +33 1 83 62 56 17<br>musee-henner.fr<br>Instagram: @museehenner | Metro: Malesherbes |

**MUSÉE BOURDELLE**
**18, RUE ANTOINE BOURDELLE**
**75015 PARIS**

Kiss

| | | |
|---|---|---|
| Mon: closed | +33 1 49 54 73 73<br>bourdelle.paris.fr<br>Instagram: @museebourdelle | Metro: Montparnasse-Bienvenüe |

# #27

## **A LUXURY HOTEL,**
## LIKE OUT IN THE COUNTRY

Tucked away in the heart of the most beautiful part of Montmartre, the Hôtel Particulier is a true gem: exquisitely tasteful, luxurious, comfortable rooms, and a garden where you can have breakfast (or more) when the weather is nice, all in a charming, romantic setting.

The hotel has just five suites, each in a different style and all magnificent!

If you can't afford to spend a night here, take advantage of the restaurant (which is open to the public) to gain access to this special place in what is one of if not the most charming areas of the city.

Go on, treat yourself!

**L'HÔTEL PARTICULIER**
**23, AVENUE JUNOT, PAVILLON D**
**75018 PARIS**

+33 1 53 41 81 40

hotelparticulier.com
Instagram: @hotelparticuliermontmartre

Metro:
Lamarck-Caulaincourt

# #28

# EXPERIENCE THE SACRED SOUL OF PARIS

France is the eldest daughter of the Catholic Church and Paris is its capital (to find out why, see our other guide to the city, *Secret Paris*).

One of the most spiritual ways to experience the city's sacred soul is by taking part in the perpetual adoration at Sacré-Cœur in Montmartre: since 1 August 1885, people have been praying in the basilica non-stop, day and night, seven days a week – including during two world wars and the Covid pandemic.

And anyone can participate. Just book your spot – by phone, online or even on site (sometimes for the same day) – and choose an option: dormitory, single or shared room (all very reasonably priced). On the day of your reservation, go to the reception before 9:30pm and sign up for at least one hour-long slot between 11pm and 7am.

**PERPETUAL ADORATION**
**AT SACRÉ-CŒUR BASILICA**
**35, RUE DU CHEVALIER DE LA BARRE**
**75018 PARIS**

+33 1 53 41 89 00

sacre-coeur-montmartre.com/hotellerie-et-groupes/lhotellerie-de-la-basilique/participer-a-une-nuit-dadoration

Metro: Abbesses

JESV GALLIA POENITENS ET DEVOTA

At 10pm there is a public mass. At 11pm, when the basilica closes, only those who have signed up for the perpetual adoration stay on. It is now time for the night of prayer before the Blessed Sacrament to begin, in an atmosphere of faith, fervour and true reverence. You can stay longer than planned, rest in your room if you're tired, come back again later or wander alone in the half-lit basilica (in silence, of course).

It's a truly magical experience for Catholics, but not only: no questions are asked at the reception. Catholics, Christians and adherents of other faiths are all welcome to come together for part of the night for this extraordinary shared experience.

When you leave the basilica in the early morning, you'll be filled with a strange sense of wellbeing.

#29

# **HAVE MONTMARTRE** ALL TO YOURSELF

Montmartre is probably our favourite district in Paris – unfortunately, it's overrun with people almost all year round. That's why we recommend this short alternative route: it will allow you to steer clear of the crowds at Place du Tertre (which should be avoided at all costs) and the Sacré-Cœur while taking you to the most authentic part of the district, still frequented by locals.

Get off the metro at Lamarck-Caulaincourt, go up the stairs and walk along Avenue Junot, one of the most beautiful in Paris. Maison Tristan Tzara (designed by Adolf Loos and built in 1926) is at No. 15. Villa Léandre (No. 23 ter) is a dead-end street with pretty, low brick houses in the Anglo-Norman style, overgrown with climbing plants. At the far end of the avenue, note the doorway to No. 4, which looks like the blades of a windmill (there used to be several windmills in the area).

At 21 Avenue Junot, Passage Lepic-Junot, in the heart of the former maquis of Montmartre, is now closed off by a gate. You have two options: either ring the intercom of the pétanque court to play a game followed by a drink at the bar, or go into the Hôtel Particulier (see page 134) for a bite to eat or a drink (starting from breakfast).

© BASTIEN NVS – UNSPLASH

Retrace your steps to 1 Avenue Junot, one of the most beautiful private residences in all of Paris. If by some miracle the door happens to open in front of you, politely ask the resident(s) if you can peek inside this fantastic spot where vines grow and rabbits frolic at the foot of the Moulin Blute-Fin.

You'll soon spot the Moulin Blute-Fin on the left, one of the last two mills in Paris along with the Moulin Radet (better known as the Moulin de la Galette), though the latter is no longer at its original location.

Walking back up the avenue on the left, make a detour to 11 Avenue Junot to see the Hameau des Artistes (Artists' Hamlet) from the outside, which links Avenue Junot to Rue Lepic (at No. 75) and is usually locked, requiring an access code to enter.

Retrace your steps to the beginning of Avenue Junot and Place Marcel Aymé, where you can spot the amusing *Le Passe-Muraille* ('The Man Who Walked through Walls'), a sculptural tribute to Aymé's novel of the same name.

As you go down Rue de l'Abreuvoir, you'll see on the right a number of houses and artists' studios nestled in a large natural park. A sort of Parisian Villa Medici, this site rents modestly priced studios (ranging from 60 to 100 square metres) to foreign artists for a year. Just below, Place Dalida has superb views of the Sacré-Cœur – probably the most panoramic views in the entire city.

In the square stands a bronze bust of the singer Dalida. You can caress her ample bosom to give it a patina to rival that of Juliet's breasts in Verona (and maybe for a bit of good luck, if you're superstitious). Then head right, up towards the vineyards. The metro is just a short walk away.

NB: The doors of 45 Rue Lepic open unexpectedly onto an alley lined with artists' and artisans' studios.

On the hill, at the heart of this itinerary, is a little-known café that is the perfect place for a break away from the crowds. Les 5 Marches serves simple, delicious dishes for lunch in a pretty setting.

**LES 5 MARCHES**
**12, RUE GIRARDON**
**75018 PARIS**

| | | |
|---|---|---|
| Closed on Thursdays | 5marches-montmartre.com<br>Instagram: @les.5.marches | Metro: Lamarck-Caulaincourt |

NICOLAS CARDON

And when you're ready for dinner after your walk, we're big fans of restaurant Adraba, on the other side of the Butte as you head down towards Pigalle. This excellent Levantine restaurant serves Middle Eastern cuisine with a very friendly welcome and a young, lively, slightly trendy atmosphere. We particularly like dining at the counter. Perfect for rounding off your day in Montmartre!

**ADRABA**
**40, RUE VÉRON**
**75018 PARIS**

+33 7 83 57 38 99

adraba-paris.com
Instagram: @adraba.paris

Metro: Abbesses

PHOTOS © BONTEMPS

# #30

# THE BEST PLACES **FOR A SWEETER SIDE OF PARIS**

Paris is the city of master pastry chefs. A stop at Pierre Hermé or Cédric Grolet is, of course, still essential, but behind these big names are countless artisans who also deserve their moment in the spotlight. Here is our selection.

> **Bontemps** (3rd and 17th arrondissements)

Now a temple of sweet Paris, Bontemps simply serves the best tarts in the city, especially its seasonal fruit tarts: blood orange and orange blossom in January, rhubarb and thyme in spring, or red plums at the start of the school year. The shop, as pretty as a charming family home, also hides a spacious, welcoming tearoom and a large terrace in the building's courtyard.

Bontemps rarely goes viral on social media, but true sugar lovers know that this is where you will be served an orgasmic shortcrust pastry, the secret of which the chef guards jealously.

| | | |
|---|---|---|
| **BONTEMPS**<br>**57, RUE DE BRETAGNE**<br>**75003 PARIS** | **23, RUE PONCELET**<br>**75017 PARIS** | Kiss |
| +33 1 42 74 10 68<br>Metro: Temple, Arts et Métiers | +33 1 53 81 01 22<br>Metro: Ternes | bontemps.paris<br>Instagram: @bontempsparis |

> **Maison Aleph** (4th and 18th arrondissements)

In the heart of the Marais, this tiny shop with its pretty blue tiles has achieved a subtle fusion. Its chef combines the aromas of her native Syria with the techniques of French pâtisserie. The result is a continuous state of bliss: pistachio and orange blossom, lemon and cardamom, mango and jasmine, or fig and cinnamon.

**MAISON ALEPH**
**20, RUE DE LA VERRERIE**
**75004 PARIS**

+33 9 83 03 42 02
Metro: Hôtel de Ville
maisonaleph.com
Instagram: @maisonaleph

**63, RUE DES ABBESSES**
**75018 PARIS**

+33 9 87 31 09 10
Metro: Blanche

> **Des Gâteaux et du Pain** (7th and 15th arrondissements)

On rue du Bac, you will find Claire Damon, the most respected pastry chef in the business. Exceptionally demanding when it comes to seasonality, she understands fruit like no one else, and her creations are always delicate and subtle, from her blackcurrant Mont Blanc to her pear and muscovado sugar tart.

**DES GÂTEAUX ET DU PAIN**
**89, RUE DU BAC**
**75007 PARIS**

Metro: Rue du Bac
desgateauxetdupain.com
Instagram:
@desgateauxetdupain.clairedamon

**63, BOULEVARD PASTEUR**
**75015 PARIS**

Metro: Gare Montparnasse

© PHILIPPE VAURES SANTA MARIA

© PHILIPPE VAURES SANTA MARIA

© SONGE

> **Songe** (10th arrondissement)

Adrien Cusson, a former analytical chemistry engineer, opened this blue-toned shop in 2025 on a quiet street near the Canal Saint-Martin. Here you will find pastries unlike anything you will see elsewhere, inspired by flavours he discovered on the other side of the world: exotic fruit and ube tart, made with a purple yam from the Philippines; corn and lulo cheese-cake, using a tangy fruit from South America; or hazelnut cake with roasted Japanese green tea, hojicha.

**SONGE**
**25, RUE JACQUES LOUVEL-TESSIER**
**75010 PARIS**

| | | |
|---|---|---|
| +33 9 83 33 90 11 | songe-patisserie.com<br>Instagram: @songe.patisserie | Metro: Goncourt |

> **Le Bon** (11th arrondissement)

One of the most talked-about addresses of the moment, Le Bon is run by a charming young couple who make some of the city's most exquisite pastries in their bright, discreet shop. Pear and pecan, black sesame and passion fruit, chocolate and hazelnut: creations for every taste, but always made with a contemporary touch and plenty of talent.

**LE BON**
**85, BOULEVARD VOLTAIRE**
**75011 PARIS**

| | | |
|---|---|---|
| +33 6 13 26 30 03 | lebonpatisserie.fr<br>Instagram: @lebon.patisserie | Metro: Voltaire |

© LE BON

> **Pleincœur** (17th arrondissement)

Maxime Frédéric, the most talented pastry chef of his generation, finally has a place of his own. Head pastry chef at the Cheval Blanc Paris hotel, in La Samaritaine, as well as for Louis Vuitton, he has created at Pleincœur a nostalgic world of old copper cake moulds on the walls and dark solid-wood details.

His pastries may look simple, but they have an uncommon elegance and are made with an unrivalled sense of balance, as in his hazelnut or vanilla desserts.

A few streets away is L'Atelier Pleincœur, where he makes his chocolates and processes his own hazelnuts, his signature product.

**PLEINCŒUR**
**64, RUE DES BATIGNOLLES**
**75017 PARIS**

pleincoeur.com
Instagram: @pleincoeur_official
Metro: Brochant

**Atelier Pleincœur**
12, rue Mstislav Rostropovitch
75017 Paris
Metro: Brochant

© AURORE NGUYEN

# THANKS

Florence Amiel, Dan Assayag, Mathilde Bargibant, Émilie de Beaumont, Kees & Aude van Beek, Emmanuel Bérard, Florent Billioud, Antoine Blachez, Philippe Bonfils, Ghislaine Bouchet, Jean-Claude Boulliard, Pierrick Bourgault, Louis-Marie Bourgeois, Jean-Baptiste Bourgeois, Marie & Brandino Brandolini, Jean-Laurent Cassely, Philippe Darmayan, Stéphane & Géraldine Decaux, Simon Edelstein, Vincent Formery, Servane & Giovanni Giol, Philippe Gloaguen, Amaël Gohier, Azmina Goulamaly, Alexandre Guérin, Ines Guérin, Patrick Haas, Elvire Haberman, Catherine Ivanichtchenko, Antoine Jonglez, Aurélie Jonglez, Louis Jonglez, Romaine Jonglez, Stéphanie & Guillaume Jonglez, Timothée & Delphine Jonglez, Benoît de Larouzière, Xavier & Sophie Lièvre, Clémence Mathé, Olivier & Valérie de Panafieu, Marianne & Fabrice Perreau-Saussine, Hélène Poulit, Alireza Razavi, Valérie Renaud, Stéphanie Rivoal, Dominique Roger, Béatrice & Pierre Rosenberg, Bertrand Saint Guilhem, Hervé Schlosser, Damien Seyrieix, François Simon, Ambroise Tézenas, Victoire & Olivier de Trogoff, Marie-Christine Valla, Delphine Valluet, Henri & Natacha Villeroy, Ézechiel Zerah.

Special thanks to Fany Péchiodat for the concept behind the collection.

**This book was created by:**
Thomas Jonglez, author
Emmanuelle Willard Toulemonde, layout
Sophie Schlondorff, translation
Janah Gough, editing
Dikshit Akbari, proofreading
Mado de La Quintinie, publishing

Cover photo: © Yaroslava Borz

You can write to us at info@jonglezpublishing.com
Follow us on Instagram at @jonglez_publishing

## From the same publisher

### Photo Books

Abandoned America: The age of Consequences
Abandoned Asylums
Abandoned Australia
Abandoned Belgium
Abandoned Churches: Unclaimed Places of Worship
Abandoned Cinemas of the World
Abandoned France
Abandoned Germany
Abandoned Lebanon
Abandoned Italy
Abandoned Japan
Abandoned Spain
Abandoned USSR
Abandoned World – An AI-generated exploration
After the Final Curtain: The Fall of the American Movie Theater
After the Final Curtain: America's Abandoned Theaters
Baikonur – Vestiges of the Soviet Space Program
Cinemas – A French Heritage
Chernobyl's Atomic Legacy – 25 years after disaster
Clickbait – A visual journey through AI-generated stories
Destination: Wellness – Our 35 best places in the world to take time out
Forbidden Places – Exploring our Abandoned Heritage
Forgotten Heritage
Oblivion
Parisian Theatres – Exceptional Venues
Secret Art Nouveau
Secret Sacred Sites
The cinemas of India – An exceptional heritage
Venice deserted
Venice from the skies

### 'Confidential' and 'Soul of' Guides

Berlin Confidential
Lisbon Confidential
Los Angeles Confidential
Malta Confidential
Marrakesh Confidential
Munich Confidential
New York Condential

Soul of Amsterdam - A guide to the 30 best experien
Soul of Athens – 30 experiences
Soul of Barcelona – 30 experiences
Soul of Brussels – A guide to exceptional experiences
Soul of Detroit – A guide to exceptional experiences
Soul of Kyoto – A guide to exceptional experiences
Soul of Marseille – A guide to exceptional experience
Soul of Milan – A guide to exceptional experiences
Soul of Rome – A guide to exceptional experiences
Soul of Tokyo – A guide to exceptional experiences
Soul of Venice – A guide to exceptional experiences
Soul of Vienna – A guide to exceptional experiences

## Atlases of curiosities

Atlas of extreme weather
Atlas of forbidden places
Atlas of geographical curiosities
Atlas of geographical curiosities – Britain
Atlas of unusual wines
Atlas of urban vineyards

## Secret atlases

Berlin – The secret atlas
London – The secret atlas
New York – The secret atlas
Paris – The secret atlas
Rome – The secret atlas
Venice – The secret atlas

## 'Secret' Guides

Secret Amsterdam
Secret Bali – An unusual guide
Secret Bangkok
Secret Barcelona
Secret Bars & Restaurants in Paris
Secret Bath – An unusual guide
Secret Belfast
Secret Berlin
Secret Boston – An unusual guide
Secret Brighton – An unusual guide
Secret Brooklyn
Secret Brussels
Secret Budapest
Secret Buenos Aires
Secret Campania
Secret Cape Town
Secret Copenhagen
Secret Corsica
Secret Dolomites
Secret Dublin – An unusual guide
Secret Edinburgh – An unusual guide
Secret Florence
Secret French Riviera
Secret Geneva
Secret Glasgow – An unusual guide
Secret Granada
Secret Helsinki
Secret Istanbul
Secret Johannesburg
Secret Kuala Lumpur
Secret Lisbon
Secret Liverpool – An unusual guide
Secret London – An unusual guide
Secret London – Unusual Bars & Restaurants
Secret Los Angeles – An unusual guide
Secret Louisiana
Secret Madrid
Secret Mexico City
Secret Milan
Secret Montreal – An unusual guide
Secret Naples
Secret New Orleans – An unusual guide
Secret New York – An unusual guide
Secret New York – Curious Activities
Secret New York – Hidden Bars & Restaurants
Secret Normandy
Secret Paris
Secret Potsdam
Secret Prague
Secret Provence
Secret Rio
Secret Rome
Secret Seville
Secret Singapore
Secret Stockholm
Secret Strasbourg
Secret Sussex – An unusual guide
Secret Tokyo
Secret Tuscany
Secret Venice
Secret Venice Lagoon
Secret Vienna
Secret Washington DC – An unusual guide
Secret York – An unusual guide

Follow us on Facebook and Instagram

Registration of copyright: September 2026 – Edition: 01
ISBN: 978-2-38715-077-6
Printed in June 2026 by Dedrax, Bulgaria